Kermit Noteboo

MW00884896

Lined Composition Notebook featuring Kermit the Frog.

The Kermit Notebook is Perfect for:

Writing, Ideas, Notetaking, Diary Entries, Planning, Organizing, To-Do Lists, Mind-Maps.

The Choice is Yours.

All work in this 'Kermit Notebook' is copyright and owned by:

Name: ....

Contact Number: ....

Email: ....

Chapter Name:	Description:	Page No:

Chapter Name:	Description:	Page No:

Chapter Name:	Description:	Page No:

Thank You

I hope that you have enjoyed using this Kermit Notebook.

Your Comments and Feedback are highly appreciated.

If you would like to leave a Review with Amazon, please find the link to this Kermit Notebook:

'Kermit Notebook' by Jonathan Shaw.

Click and scroll down to where you will be able to leave a review.

Thank you in advance, I look forward to hearing from you.

Jonathan Shaw

Made in the USA
Columbia, SC
16 December 2019

84955786R00063